This Pageant Preparation Journal Belongs To:

Congratulations on preparing for your pageant! As you embark on this journey, think about how to develop and execute your winning strategy. Set a goal, create a plan, and focus on your unique gifts. Don't forget to have fun, embrace your authentic self, and be confident.
You are a Queen!

- *Desiree Roberts*

Copyright © 2021 by Desiree Roberts. All rights reserved.

Pageant Overview

Pageant Goals

Pageant Checklist

Pageant Budget

Pageant Sponsorship

Important Dates

Pageant Resume

Personal Introduction

Interview

Platform

Community Service & Involvement

Appearances

Social Media

Wardrobe

Hair & Makeup

Coaching Notes

Made in the USA
Columbia, SC
18 June 2021